HOLD TIGHT: THE TRUCK DARLING POEMS

Jeni Olin

HOLD TIGHT:
THE TRUCK DARLING POEMS

Jeni Olin

Hanging Loose Press
Brooklyn, New York

Published by Hanging Loose Press, 231 Wyckoff Street, Brooklyn, New York 11217. All Rights Reserved. No part of this book may be reproduced without the publisher's written permission, except for brief quotations in reviews.

www.hangingloosepress.com

Printed in the United States of America
10 9 8 7 6 5 4 3 2 1

Hanging Loose thanks the Literature Program of the New York State Council on the Arts for a grant in support of the publication of this book.

Cover art and design by Donna Brook and Marie Carter

Acknowledgments: Some of these poems first appeared in *The Boog Portable Reader, Hanging Loose* and *Lit*. The poems in section III were published as a chapbook, *The Pill Book*, by Faux Press, Cambridge, Massachusetts.

Library of Congress Cataloging-in-Publication Data available on requestion.

 Produced at The Print Center, Inc. 225 Varick St., New York, NY 10014, a non-profit facility for literary and arts-related publications. (212) 206-8465

GUTS

I. SO COLD YOU COULD FENCE WITH YOUR NIPPLES

II. SANS VISA SANS CULOTTES

III. THE PILL BOOK

IV. LIKE A LAKE TOUCHING 4 STATES BUT NOT GETTING ANY OF THEM WET

For my shrink, who believes in what I have to offer.

And in fierce and loyal memory of Darragh Park,
who was never meant for this world anyway.

SO COLD YOU COULD FENCE
WITH YOUR NIPPLES

ARTIST'S STATEMENT:

I care deeply for child society.
I am into grief, porn, & denim.
Sensations of vertigo & disorder
are sources of pleasure for me.
I am interested in repossession of my soul.
I know what doesn't work.
I want my work to comfort
brain-damaged kids & soulsick adults.
I hold no currency in the adult world,
but no tenancy in the child one.
If I were to choreograph
movement to my heartbreak,
it would be a flock of adults flying over me,
wearing T-shirts that read,
"You are loved. Relax, Kiddo."

AFTERMATH

for Todd Colby

Something ethical is moving me
away from your beauty. For serious.
You rage like swollen math & allergies
in my brain. In my dreams I am hatching
the hot eggs of black oceanographers.
The massive animal flu of love
has run me down. I am running
the temperature of a star in a ditch.
I inherit other people's dreams
when I'm crushed out on them.
Are you so strong or is it the Black Russian in me?
Can I french you where it hurts one more time
this time with apathy?
Sushi'd out & despairingly acoustic, you
cannot bring sexy back without a receipt.
Hot little animal, hold tight.

THE REST IS NOISE

for Darragh Park, again

*"When you're black & blue it's time to
take a holiday."*

Hey little flutter in mon coeur, I stand alone
in some grief-sponged shadow & nap in the halfway
Hamptons house of a phantom-loving embrace.
I want to be an anime angel, to go on as a balmy
robot would be indelicate I'm thinking. I am not
a reformer but I am not allied with pain anymore.
I am a straight boi in the arts who has discovered
& admitted I cannot control who loves me & who
never will. I have learned I must live without this
love to avoid bruising everyone I touch. I will live
on whey protein & great masterful music is the plan.
A water draftsman of faint lawns turned me on
to Rufskin jeans with the cheeks cut out
& The Band & the safety fail of leaving
milkweed to freeze with Two Serious Ladies
out back. This dreamy blade eats only carbs & lives
alone on iced ginger beer, urging me to close my eyes
during a time out & float into a sour milk classroom
under the hirsute anthems of Giacinto Scelsi.
Aw, shucks, dearheart, you know I'd love to but
I'm just listening on a 4th grade level these days.

I KNOW YOU'RE MARRIED BUT I HAVE FEELINGS TOO.

Far from your democracy,
romance can flourish
beneath the switchbacks
of the Roosevelt Island tram.

Still, I am not to be fooled
by athletic lovemaking,
long cars, or Taco Bell.
Like those kids grabbing for

frosting-bag teats in National
Geographic, I know exactly what
I am going for. Better check your pulse
card exactly since I am going for that too.

A HARD DAY'S NIGHT OF THE LIVING DEAD

Don't Look Back, the Morton Salt Girl
cried, "there's a bad moon on the rise..."
which I do not think happens anywhere
in Sofia Coppola's film The Virgin Suicides,
I do not think it happens anywhere
else, but maybe it's the trees in my lungs,
it's not the Dexedrine. Receding, I pop
a black beauty & then another & so on
& now I am Young, Gifted, & Black.
Canonized? Maybe. I expire on the tiny punk
heart of the Crab Nebula. How many
heartsprains & how many bloody drumsticks
we just can't stop gnawing on? Here
we rage bereft, everyone is passing
on, but in Paradise no one is passing
gas, everyone finally relieved. Ah Verona!
If there were only some kind of future & not
just sexy grammar shouted from the marshes.
Fill me up with Premium. Feverish, fibrous
& generally trying not to die, I need guidance
with Heaven just a seizure-alert dog
on an invisible lead. This, our weepy
bloated saga so natural but then
the sun is natural & so is tobacco.

AND A KIND OF MORAL AUTISM SETTLES

for Vincent Katz

On a catwalk always lead with your heart.
In a duet of arpeggios & trills, morose girls
slumped against things. Ineffable beauty.
A flotilla of fanfare in smashed daylight
& Kate Moss's collarbone sticks up as reassuringly
as a barf bag on a bumpy flight.
I intercept many a thought Heaven meant for another boi.
I am as faithful as a seahorse or as Marianne.
I am the hand up the Mona Lisa's skirt.
I tattoo a wall socket on my bicep
just to feel "alive" I feel sometimes I am "dying"
aesthetically never mind morally
which is pretty suckful like the dead French
I once loved in textbooks on blond executive paper,
the starboard side of hope. It pained me awfully
to accept their art in the Swabian line
of violence as when, "a constellation passes
over, alas, cardiologists."

CAN YOU SMELL MY CAVITIES?

The wallflowers expect no relief efforts
anymore & unrequited lust sucks but
commitment is stifling like having a sinus
cold in a costume somewhere anywhere you
really don't want to be while really
feeling for Darfur but not saying something
anything at some party. Awkward!

THINGS ARE GOING TO CHANGE I CAN FEEL IT.

Thanks to Mayakovsky, suicide notes are harder to write.
That's a scream & I feel about as safe & humane
as Diane Arbus or invisible canine fencing.
I took the Facebook "Are you a good person?" quiz
& the result is: You are a good person.
Chest-deep in swampy terrain, I ship my corpse quickly
with a tracking number because I want positive feedback.
With a Murphy-bed fear of entrapment,
when he screams at me in my dreams his language
is like an enema lesson I study dutifully.
Prelapsarian like, "Here I am in the foliage, keep away!"
but post-Fall during my Gap Year abroad undid me
& she didn't stay for muesli in the morning.
So anyway I emailed you I'd be dead tonight.
I cleaned out my brush to make you angel hair pasta.
"Word out on the street is you've gone starving,"
but I can't spot even one ab in The State I Am In.

THE MILKY IMPULSE TO KISS & BE FRIENDS

Of all the gin joints in the world, you
have to dress strategically to be safe
at the Braille cathouse where everybody
feels everything. The Lebanese Blonde
broke down, broke the bank, I'm so Baroque.
My JDate moniker is StickAForkInMe
& I bleed through in watercolors.
In the cafeteria of the gruntingly sordid,
a monk saunters suggestively by,
completely cable-free
with an integrated touchpad,
& blanches on the playground
at the Reservoir. Now he's chillin'
inside a soul-sized sunburn. I'm over.
Like a nude descending an escalator,
I need a guardian cherub to nurse me
with beer & tripe in Jamaica.

PASSING CUSTOMS

Aw, you lose your corsage, Mother Courage
amidst unopened Sponsor Child mail. Tiny fists
pummel the cherubs who cruise this ashen noon.
I have a soft spot for fondling myself to fruition

on the Autobahn. Like a Vespa-riding Casanova,
me & my musketeer come faster than Christmas.
As the wind jerks the rain back & forth
with its hundred fangs, the Chrysler glistens,

a tin foil asparagus spear. Something
from Bright Eyes has me sleeping in clouds
of fire the way maybe the sun naps. Perhaps
it is "the hue of the sun caught flying":

a Kodachrome palette of sashimi colors
with cocaine, comic distance & a flourish
of burgeoning typologies. It is misting
on the mountains at the flood relief concerts.

Naturally it is snowing in the cafeteria
where you live. A scale model on display
beneath heat lamps of an emotional version
of continental drift greets lunch kids,

hungry for the scene the kiss demanded,
while a rhizome of rain plainly is just
a tear falling on spectator pumps.
I keep shorting out my ankle monitor.

I text vote for American Idol yet I've nothing
to declare entering your country, pierced
with bright flames, Norman fury. I used to think
I was elitist now I just think I am an alien.

THE TEMPTATION TO EXIST

for Jim Behrle
a Christmas poem

There, there, Sweet Pea, put DOWN the gun,
hotter than under a flamenco dancer's dress,
you buckle my knees with unbridled longing
& every time I see your face, an angel gets laid
at the Rose Parade. It is so cold you could fence
with your nipples & glacially between us, in sand
the shade of British teeth in sepia Glamour Shots,
the reindeer faint before the flaming gates
or just maybe my heart needs
a polygraph so it can lie
still.

I JUST BURNT MY NECK WITH A CURLING IRON, PROMISE!

for David Wojnarowicz

I think lovers should sport calorie info badges
so you know just how much love you're consuming.
Exhumed, I want a star sticker next to my name
when Saint Peter does roll call to find MySpace
templates for the variety of clavicles available
to "bling up" the angels with hickeys
in the bondage bardo. If I could knit my nerves
together into one furious anthem, I'd make you
a soprano with the ease of starlings
who know the birthday of every thermal
passing through the Mission. This is sick
& horny but also I wish I were more heathen
& less confused & had a dick so David Wojnarowicz
would bring me home, spent & dehydrated,
ruffle my manga dreds, sighing: Be courageous,
Sugartits, & marry yourself.

PSYCHE'S LAMENT

Left behind in remedial mondo
living when everybody's graduated
cum laude to flash fantasy, chasing

Eros is a tough love job for a tryst
aficionado drumming up trade
in a porn-set hamlet chock-full

of eunuchs popping antidepressants.
Underscored with the sinister
2-note organ riff to the tune of

It's a Dirty Job But Somebody
Has To Do It. And that Revelations
biz at the end? Like frat boys,

loud cries & we rushed together—
that was all.

HIS & HERS URINALS

My sanity calls the bitch of your imagination
home after dark. Your friendly neighborhood
matzoh ball retriever – it misses you!
If you were to iron the linen MapQuest
to your heart, kid, I'd still get there anyway
because I am an expert flatliner, duh.
You squeeze your retinas so tight to shut
me out as a monk's hymen in the Mojave.
You are dehydrated & failing but germane to my lust.
The snow tribes are flexing their Smurf-blue
muscles for free which is how exposed
I'd strain to be for you in heat.
The Birdwell Sea Britches are next to go
on our ice floe, the crystal salt chunks
pressed in the shape of newt tongues.
The western mountain ranges rage, mere cutouts
of the tantric positions that unscrew
me when I think of you, holding me aloft
in your temples while holding her inside
with a Smith & Wesson against The Temple
of the Golden Pavilion, i.e. your thighs
as seen through an amber honey jar
of stale piss. You've gotten lazy & deranged.

MERE FOOD TUBES LIVING IN ISOLATION

for Steven Abrams

I can't help but notice you have nice irises
pimped with light. I feel so deeply but can't
show up. I am always reassuring people I am
not who I say I am. I can't help but think
if the mummies at the Met had been massaged

with the pearl jam of Kiehl's, things might
have turned out differently. Cryogenics
should really be the study of tears
at icy altitudes like frozen eyegum
on a widow nobody has brought inside

or dewdrops on a Pabst Blue Ribbon
sweating inside the fridge. I kneel
so steeply but can't throw up. I have to turn
my "main squeeze" over so tightly to get even
1 last drop like a dry toothpaste tube

curled as starkly as an anorexic 8th grader's
pen & ink diagram of the human inner ear,
like a wax one. My hairstylist says to lubricate
my extensions, but everybody's trying to do that
anyway, everybody bawling to lube the planet

against extinction, but I need an extension,
like a tax one, I mean, like a less taxing one.
I peel so deeply but can't grow up.

SPOONING

I aspire to a celebration of dust
but my shrink has other plans:
"If you worked harder, you could
remake Vincent Gallo films."
I play well with others but
the damselflies grow hysterical
anyway. Wouldn't it be touching
to try on people at a sample sale?
I am always chasing a better fit
& then staggering forward to pay
dearly for something I don't even want.
Trusting hyperrealism, trusting scum,
I find the droppings of white men
are brown in a fetal curl.

THE KINDLE 2 WAS A GIFT!

Nothing's more infuriating than mental luxury
without a system. I sound like a.m. radio.
Still, I'd rather be lush, melancholy, & tart
than boring & pedantic. Rather let my feelings
run amuck or "limp amuck" in my case. Rather
grin endearingly falling into a decline. Little
dried islands of blemish makeup like croissant flakes,
all tragically flawed, makes me think of some great dancer
who nevertheless has thick legs. And tea-oil toothpicks
tingle like antiseptic on Nancy Reagan's legs. Me,
I said, "No" to drugs years before the First Family
visited the Taj Mahal, rising from the pollution mist
which is not meant for North Americans? After all,
there is an innate intelligence to the universe.
Nursing invalids from hot countries, I need a poem
that breathes like a red herring needs a Triumph
on a tax-free paradise isle. My mom is vast & handsome,
flies all the time to the Amalfi Coast, with low visibility,
knows nothing of my corpuscular wretchedness. Me?
I had the foresight to buy an iPod at age 8. Speaking
of turbulence, Eileen Myles looks like a Kennedy.

SLOW DOWN, KILLER.

for D.D.

Feral grace, to work out our own tiny salvations
by fear & trembling. I believe we put ourselves
into this State of Grace. Beyond post-swim hygiene
& antique weaponry, I believe the philistines really
missed out on what I have to offer. "At that point
where one may say Emergency & mean Time," I need
a defibrillator on the corpse of my libido. Sometimes
I think I am horny when I just need to go to the bathroom.
Sometimes I just need to go to the bathroom & stay there
on days it is so hard to shout myself away from death.
But if you could remove the lampshades off my lust,
I could safely glide us in. We need to get back.
You know what I mean.

WELCOME TO COSTCO. I LOVE YOU.

I am a library of tears about to check out
Bromancing the Stone. I got more monkeys on my back
than the Rock of Gibraltor. Isn't it crazy
that last night a deejay saved my lyfe
with The Weakness in Me, that Sakharov created
the bomb & that we chew on each other's genitals?
I suffer accelerations that are vicious & unnerving:
I feel G Star-raw when I french my doorman.
I excel at graff bombing because of my paste-ups.
Downing pale ales & downy pale males,
I can teach you the Rohypnol Shuffle.
Let's train out here with the binging banana fish.
I stick out as lushly as the live one in a snuff clip,
or the shock of red butter between the legs of a 9 year old
sobbing over Tiger Beat, subtitled: Aw, her first rape.
The sign of the OMG = the puree of crime.
I guess I just love the idea of stage directions
for the heart when it is sick. I am weird. I think
break-up emails should only be allowed to happen
underwater like aquabirth. When you pulled me up
under my armpits, I thought you were trying to stretch me,
not help me bleaken a Mother's Day.

MISTER PHOTOGRAPHER, I'M READY FOR MY CLOSE-UP.

Unpasteurized & on time, your anatomy
seems not bad at all. Getting on gorgeously,
Commander, this pulsing envelope,
filled with grief & snot, LOVES YOU.
If I die, this nonlove continues anyway
& I've boned up for my post-mortem exam
with the hygiene of G.G. Allin,
doused with Shalimar & brainily snorting air
in the Alps. Breathless, the white tufts of edelweiss
in these sweet, sweet nerves
shooting through my stomach,
sprouting all around.

AOI HANA: MY BLUE HEAVEN

for Elliott Smith

A lady of the night with a heart of rose gold, I feel
like shit the morning after. The Morning After
Pill too many calories to chase down, I'd rather
just flush some child. The doctors remain calm
around my EKG which bounces around like the liner notes
for Peanuts, less cologne. But keep the paddles ready.
The Post-it note did not stick to my rib cage,
damn. I enjoy people visually but I need an intervention.
I'm not manic, I just have a lot to say, starting with
Don't Fear the Reaper & dying with, More Cowbell.
I lost my safety net today & now I am losing my mind.
This soul is not obscene, but this soul is not my scene.
This birth certificate crawlingly yours, Sweet Saint Jude.
Though I only wear infant pearl chokers at night, I can't
breathe. So what will it be? I noticed you are wearing a shirt,
why? Please open your shirt so I may lay down my rod & staff,
comforted. The Dominicans are going to come
when you are fast asleep. I don't want to see
what they've done to you. Where's Method & Ghost?
Wait, why are we screwed and who is doing it? I'm on fire
for the world through the lens of a sterile Eskimo.
The courage campaign, a wild goose chase
fueled by grief. Keep the Car Running
& the Grand Prix is ours, little salt doll.
In the future I will only post in the morning.

STADIUMS OF THE PAST

Drawn & quartered, I'll fuse again,
my spine creamy. Among the icicles,
he reduces me to the size of 1/100th of a gnat
smeared like hoisin sauce on the pinky
toenail of a Barbie doll basking in, like,
Madison Square Garden, i.e. he sooo trivializes
my animal pain. Inhaling my Grasshopper,
I am turning back to my Nashville Pussy,
The Weakness in Me, High as Hell, Crazy
He Calls Me, Something He Can Feel.

CASUALTY PLUS

When will I see you again, when will we share
precious moments of a smudged man-child slipping
softly into Truffaut's cold sheets? Lightning

is striking me as I leak this. You are striking too,
like The Temptations, there is a chapel in the pines
waiting for us around the bend, sayeth an Eagle Scout,

staining The Way of the Peaceful Warrior
with wet dreams. I'm soaking, spinning on Delicate,
I'm on Rinse. Rapid cycling — I live there.

Can you undie someone? Rit-red, the danger of frostbite
never behind us like soft surrender snapping at our spurs.
We are Texans, thoroughbreds of a good vintage.

We royals eat our veggies, hold tight, & avoid the heat.
Through the commonwealth tenure of 3 queer boyfriends,
I put up with a lot. Well that hurts. I'll do it but

that hurts. My laptop keeps freezing on me
& my default key for pressing on is sticky
with delays up to more than 5 hours. I know

the expiration date of the world, when it will go bad,
but you will have to tongue wrestle me into oblivion
to get it & why would you want it anyway?

Are you sick? Are you suffering from loss
of appetite, fatigue, or decompression?
Isn't it enough we are losing in numbers like Sudoku?

Lice & glue stuck in the toupees of simply the best
we have, effective for boarding immediately. The living
get First Priority. Are you fucking kidding me?

PENICILLIN FOR THE SMILE TRAIN

My fever's soaring, my system's down.
Delirious Militant, kiss me. I know this
place where we can hurt each other safely
with speed, like an auto whizzing through
the center of the world's largest redwood
tree, bragging. Nothing dying. Ripped Nagahyde
camouflages me against Indian Myths To Live.
Bye! Bienvenido! Uh, room #15 vacant? Post
Angelina salt & collagen adverts, we can't
help contain the swine contagion any more
than we can help those cleft-palette orphans
enjoy a mirror, mouths dented in like the squeeze
of an angry nutcracker around, say a walnut
which is really just a dried ferret brain
which really holds more emotion dead even than
a girl's groin nodule can ever feel, even infected,
even on Mexican speedballs, even pulsing quickly.

SANS VISA SANS CULOTTES

PILLOW TALK

As an insomniac compulsively flips a pillow
to cool the cheek, I turn you over again & again
& again in my mind when I need the cold side
of the said affair to rail against
"the ruinous work of nostalgia."
If life imitates art, then each stillborn
has its own mucus-bright Blue Period.
Sharks keep moving to prevent dying.
People keep moving too, unwittingly staving off
the comfort of stasis, the virility of expiration, blah, blah...
But Death, the great highlighter, makes us all shine
a bit more dearly. I'm a widowchild who needs sunblock
against your blinding legacy. I used to get my cardio up
by just sleeping next to you. In a sane world,
I'd be bumped off to warn the others of a sky
so blue at the end of the working business day
if your veins hadn't stolen the purest
Pearl Paint blue first. A broken thoroughbred –
I need a passport & vertigo pills to reach you.
Godspeed, galloping into your Misty Blue
OMG I miss you.

HAPPY HOUR

My Darling, My Hamburger, to which pageant
you parade my luminous modern pain,
you deserve the crown from The Golden Arches, son.
Heavenly bodies nudge me when I start to pass out.
Is putting a loved one out of animal pain
the same as putting them to sleep?
Nearly minimal, I ascend into vision.
Surface to Air: The Great Clearance.
"...And she's bawling. I hope to bring her home soon
beneath the heat of terrestrial sluices.
Regards,
The Great American Hero"

I SUMMITED BEA ARTHUR & ALL I GOT WAS THIS LOUSY T-SHIRT.

God, kiss me I'm a mistletoe magnet
"succumbing to the disorderly shelf
lyfe of Tampax in June." All the taste
I have is in somebody else's mouth.
My mouth your most flammable polyesther
catalyst to harden you beneath your
singed Imitation of Christ slacks.
Jeepers! You're wrecked in the fever
of high style tonight. But if you're
going to drive drunk, sigh, be sure
you have a car or at least let me
test drive your Infiniti home.
It won't backfire— such an expert buffer,
I can marshmallow lightning bolts with my
soft Gentile eyes. I am a professional
in human waste management. My aunt
has a pillow that says, "Veni, Vidi,
Velcro,"...we came, we saw, we stuck
around. That kills me.

ANYHOO

Talk scary, I understand my grace
& folly better now I know my vocation
& what I owe this lyfe for putting up
with my antics when we're all so very
tired. I have never stood expressionless,
gaping. You know that, sigh, it's all just anger
& mayonnaise anyway. Resigned to virgin
parasol drinks, I've survived every betrayal
against my cardinal love except the last:
my filthy True Religions & my diaphragm
right out there on the lawn of literature,
on the very grounds everybody's undertaking.

BIRTHDAY POEM
4/3/74 - ?

These days I want my "delicate" friends in chalk
or crapped out on a tidal crag. Black horseflies
lighting, I want nothing for my birthday unless
it's purple or blue Chronic. I splurge on tri-color
sushi for one day when the Great Pink What claims me, reluctantly
admits me to the Soul Asylum. The high
ones flap their feathery biceps through clouds
of Jupiter, "faster than a 10 year old virgin
running, chased through the South." Too young
to be dated, too old to go steady in the polar
folly heralding the dying middle-aged child.
At Vertigo, a spasm ruptures a deposit of plaque.
My cavities need to be filled. But tonight,
"this night," my teeth, tropical black diamonds
pushing off the bestial launch towards okayness
as some cheap Mex dilates my pupils, posturing
them towards death because of everything
that happened, because of everything that didn't.
Is Anybody Out There? This fog is crazy deep,
my hamstrings — weak. I am at my bottom.
I can touch the bottom! I'm almost home?
"Aw, you're just being punked on your birthday.
You're standing on a sand bar, Honey."

DO THESE HIGHLIGHTS LOOK "NATURAL" OR "EDITORIAL?"

Pacific & time-sensitive from The Pearl Rim,
my groom is stuck in the mail. At this rate,
I'm going to be like Daniel Johnston in no time.
I wish I convulsed beneath sun petals on Strong Place.
All out of Smart Water, I smashed my piggy bank today.
I leave the house with both the toaster & your lyfe
support left on because I'm cool like that.
The glandular heart is surrounded by tissue.
Though my heart is M.I.A.,
I am surrounded by tissue, also.

TRAGICALLY FLAWED IS SO 2009, LA.

for Laurence

I find Clinton's bulbous tuna-red snout wicked
hot in an obvious way. I rouge my own pixie nose
& not just at Christmas or after having coke with you,
but each day before I leave my compound breathlessly
hoping it looks like Aspen skiburn,
or the said beta reindeer, which reminds me,
every time I rock my Diesel Underoos,
how some stalker dude commented me,
"It's about time somebody celebrated
the achievements of Rudolf Christian Karl Diesel,
last seen alive September 29, 1913, an inventor
& mechanical engineer, famous for the invention
of the diesel engine. And of course he made it so it
could run on peanut oil, cooking oil, or pretty much
anything a bit oily." I could use some WD-40 for
your love, Tough Love like if I asked you for a towel
& you handed me a pissed-off jellyfish or
the placard at my wedding seat that reads:
"Rod Stewart forever cheapened morning
whiskers on antique wives. Sit here, please,
& try not to spill anything, Little MILF."

PREMATURELY GAY

"I bang cock in Bangkok." - Ludakris
"This is getting alarming." - Samuel Beckett

I loved a dreamy hustler who called his snatch
a Hitler cookie almost shyly I thought? Screaming
through the sunroof, "Only my shrink knows for sure!"
inside his Saturn, "no, not the car, but everywhere we are!"
With the 40 in the freezer, conch defrosting de-spined,
every week is menstrual shark week in our Sandals affair.
I will never bleed & I will never kneel for you,
but I will stand erect, trembling, knees buckling,
no shame, now, past, or ever. My eyes burn brightly
& when they no longer can, then the rest of me will burn, proudly like
a Buddhist monk in self-imolation
or a boy's cheeks, trying on his father's training bra
in a closet mirror. I put up with a lot & will,
until claimed by my rightful, well, no one owns me,
though the smart money is on Clooney. With the merriment
of Banquo's ghost with a cold, when you enter the casino,
I expect, demand personal loss. The Milky Way pats me
on the ass like, "Oh there, now, now, Kid. People
in a crowd aren't really like petals on a wet black bough."
So you spend your time banging your head against that.
But in a jury of your peers, you have the right to remain awesome,
heartbroken, crazy strong, maybe.

DOLL STEAK

Do your sinuses itch, little wolf,
like boys in steamy ghettos beaming
handsomely with sinister little dolls,
racked, trembling with nightsweats,
all the coloring books streaked with piss?
Like snow on bones in the Quadrangle,
I will cover you so you can begin to unlove me.
Engineered against the remarkable,
plunging, brakeless, I think you're resisting
with the rasp of 900 cigarettes in an anise eternity.
Your husky Kathleen Turner voice—
achieved via the padded rooms
of primal scream therapy & Jagermeister.
It's what nullity & rapture would sound like,
if they wailed too much. In the electron-starred vistas
of girldom, breasts are just dough balls. Swollen,
the grave, salty gulf between Linus & the blanket
skirts the black lungs of life.
"The weight of the world is love" &
you've gained weight I'm thinking.

SUBURBAN RHAPSODY

My lifeguard sports flesh flies in a coma,
collapsing new bathers back to nature.
I smoke crack because aspirin makes me write
stupid things. In cursive, Cousin, I'm swollen
& gorgeous. But I'm not linear. I hate it
when my friends wane lyrical, fiercely
sketching diagrams for how to set a broken
lyfe. Even hybrid-picking the bass line
of my trashola heart leaves only the faint
impression of a yellow carbon receipt
signed by some diabetic, pre-Snickers fix
with a dying pen in bald sunlight on a windy day.
Is your credit score stopping you from receiving
a free lap dance? Do you suffer from loss
of Appetite For Destruction, heartsprain,
fish curry & a feeling that everything
actually matters anyway? Do you experience
navy butterflies in your abdomen? Do you
hear the screams of the Kurds when your washing
machine spins too high in the final rinse cycle
or the death rattles of Darfur when you
leave loose nickels in the dryer? You might be
suffering from depression.

SLEEPING OUR WAY TO THE MIDDLE

Since I unwittingly advertise shame
on a quotidian basis, I need a class
in Defensive Living. "It was just a slip.
Why would you belabor a slip?"
"The glue hardens inside the hero
when the lights are out."
(I am the hero & you are the slip here.)
A player is a fragile thing
in hot beds of feudal hostility,
my nobility insecure because I am a trust fund fetus
with an expired D.A.R. membership.
But at Platinum Angel status, my friend's been
"saving people with light" since 1999
& doesn't know light is quick & dead
to the quick & dead, though when "casting down,"
he means well, feels deeply. Anyhoo, everybody
speaks English to stop jumpers, no resentment.

IT WAS A RECOGNIZABLE FIRE WAS IT?

The organs jump at the end of their mauve adolescence.
I am jumping into the koi pond with all my clothes on.
It's convenient to be impervious to warmth in hell
everywhere we are. And you can tell by the look on her
face, Helen Keller fingered doilies of lace with casual
carnality. Parachutists glide softly down to give me
back my Golden Arm & Hammer. The snow leopard, dirty
rich knowing we're just meat sculptures clothed in
bronzing foam, lowers its eyes, offers tenderly
an aloha speech to our exposed citizenry:
I dream about wires.
Even Jell-O scratches me.
The chewy depressants lush me out
& I've totally blown my entrance.

LEONARD, JUST SO YOU KNOW

Threatening this blood purity by overbreeding
pain, I named a benign but taxing ulcer after
you. I want to unionize the dirty aftermath.
You need a boy apron for this & I need some
girl beer goggles. You are handsome because I
want to get laid. Our war just ended because I
want to get laid. The police snipers & weeping
willows have started to claim me. I am raising
great angry children on the lawns of Europe.
The miracles begin to happen fashionably.
I've just enough breath to tell them.
I can hardly bear to understand that.
Then you take my breath away
via strangulation or something.
No problem.
You lower your eyes, pure as New York snow.
I miss nothing.
You ballet finger me with Mach 3 blades.
I noticed that too.

VICTORIA'S SECRET

To all my readers behind bars: I love you,
feel you, I do. The "martini & a piece of toast" diet
works because people feel more for beautiful friends.
Flunking nutrition (not to mention demands of shape)
Love's my lazy doll steak. I'll take a stab at it.
And you not once properly impaled. Anyhow,
I wish Texas was a country again with a tearful
Cool Hand Luke burping eggs in the deep blue
flaming dark. I could be held saline-aloft
by his teardrops, these teardrops buoy me up.
Although the days are wicked calm I keep
a sharp needle & a crash pad anyway. Thanks
for the squatter's rights to your soul but it's getting
crowded in your holding cell, getting toasty & boyish,
fever water-mark brown & rising.

POEMS, KLEENEX, & THREE MISGIVINGS

O flaked ice, I'm so lost without my Maker's Mark.
Angina, transport me into a private room at last
to take the corner off of today, smeared with
the heart tissue of angels, Live! With the tweezers
of tiny heroes, pull Apollo crabmeat from the legs
of the Breakdown Republic – anemic royalty hurling
a full Coors at America, auburn curls wicked tight
& cheekbones flushed with tidy adventure. A plague
on both your brownstones! I can feel this elite
in the Ethers & in the land of Coca-Cola, but tonight
I was "corrected" at the gym & felt shame. A column
of coral flame shot up like Vikings with powder room
vapors, starkers (blush!) amid the puffy axioms
of existence. Made stiff by the Krypton syrup in all
I touch that blossoms into the cold sick throb of
"WTF are you trying to do? WTF are you trying to do?"
I know nothing I have nothing I got nothing to say but
"I carelessly build a creepy future lyfe."

THE MISTER OF ART

I embalm the tampons because uniformity
satisfies me but I am not writing this
as a suffragist, but as a human being
mainlining Vita Plus in my tiny sensate arm,
going to the bathroom regularly but
murderously unhappy on a captain's bunk
bed, swollen & drunk in a private curl
while the moon gambles over my body
& sandwiches dot the cypress forest
leading me, with the navigational skills
of Magellan on Meth, to the public bath
where your lads were schooled last night,
like picking up a kid marked "Death"
& a kid marked "Lyfe" & banging them
together to unite this rightful firmament,
bristling with tough little hairs or like
a Gotham dawn, all stubbled with buildings.
You're the kind of person who is a successful
grisly bunny when on top. A bottom in a communal
house, I'd like you to beat me with someone
else, hissing, "You only have this:
pornography & submission & blackness & death!
You're like a faggot!" Duh! I mean, yeah,
there's rooster pills & economics, but there's
other ways to be a loving person.

VANISHING POINT

I think it would be mad sexy
if somebody hired me
to run away from them
while they stood & watched me
disappear forever. Pro bono.

LIKE VICTORIAN VILLAINS

Scalped & never meant for this world anyway,
I am summering gaily in hell as I write this.
The green blood of flora, your aorta
aching in the frieze of the execution,
the world's leafy aerial on fire. My night
naps in a children's zoo of loose hair & you're
rigid with couture in the shoulder season.
Celebrate loss in black-tie & often. The cruel
arc of your shrunken tux, camel toed in bas-relief.
That I must do these things for you to find
the fortune cookie that says, "Don't kill."
Your soul is underage at Red Lobster
but you're, like, 900 in ferret years.
My eyes green, hot & true like lobster eggs
when I'm cracked open. I think this recommends me.
I don't understand I am skinny & cool & brilliant
& want just this 1 thing why won't you give it to me?
That's just gay. When you strike again, think of
bas-relief & murder & me, why don't you?

HUNTING ACCIDENT

for Larry Clark

You make me feel like I was dying in an iron lung
& an angel dropped a ribbon-tied pony keg of nitrous
on my chest on Valentine's Day.
The accurate lust in your eyes will land us on Page Six
but still I will mount without saying sorry
because I am not a twink.
A ragged kid of science fuels my ink cartridge.
On prom night, he toasts me:
"Come on Patoots, don't make me go it alone.
I'll go mad, mad, I tell you."
Crowded in the clouds, I feel virile
like an alpha lemming shouting, "Next!"
Let me sign you in to my elite hell
& pin a pass to your nipple, your lunch money,
as pubescents in heat tag each other
in & out of algebra, gasping and symmetrical.
Your uncle hates my skate rat bangs,
that mark of suffering on a calloused night
against a heart that doesn't ice the lemmings out.
I took the bullet meant for this, your phantom heart.
You allied with the smoking Beretta, whatever.
But I would die for you not because I am loyal
but because I don't mind.

I ONLY DATE BLOODS.

Dixie-cup tits enflamed,
I threw up at my coronation.
Peeling your teardrop sticker
off my black kindergarten heart,
I was so close to being okay today.
I am changing my name to Precious Metal.
I want to be heavenly wrong, wept out.
This braided heart: reassuringly American.
I am really living in a non-Emo way.
But I'm lost here. These places.
Still it's okay to say goddamn
around the child of my grief.

DEFAULT

I love you more
than you love me
just by loving you
at all.

ON THE HEIGHTS OF DESPAIR

No longer lyrical but claustrophobic, muscle
has cleared my mind. My skull in the Football War
smokin' hot with post-hoc agony. I feel redeemed
by vulgarity on a nanosecond basis which is why
I keep porn on speed dial. I love video cleaner
when I visit & you are a fudge blur of pulsations.
Cool. A large cherry phosphate with red dye #2
for 35k a night. Lookit, your dry heaves
are bells knelling for a dead pet grief
on the shoulder, clean & auctionable. Triplets
& Miss Crummy, music, please. I don't know if
you think of me as a mistress or bereaved child.
I spend myself ahead of God when I look at you
in Norman Rockwell bug lighting. I have a black wisdom
tooth & Whoosh! I have enough time to hurt you forever!

DAYS AT SEA

Treading water in the kitchen, I cannot continue
to involve people in my tragedy – it's rude.
Joy + Britney = murder 4 lyfe.
We're not suspected & we're not dismissed, la.
You're too fat for the eternal casting;
me, too Auschwitzy-thin. In a still life
with monsters, we fight over the purple
heart I know I have lost. Anne Waldman,
please pass the Dexedrine I know I have lost.
I know I have lost. I mean really.
In an echo chamber, the angel should not feel
such pressure & fresh out of sunshine,
there's always death. These sunbeams have
got a Swede to replace me in my darkest hour.
These sunbeams are closing in, closer.
I can't go on/I won't go on/I go on.
I just don't know what happened.
OMG. OMG. OMG. If nothing, the rain comes
to break the heat of the heart. Wishing
you oranges, rifles, & thunderstorms for Easter.
The weather is — here. Wish you were — beautiful.
But at least you are having a good time on my trip.

kisses,
Truck

GOOD KETCHUP VIOLENCE

My bartending instructor didn't explain
The Screaming Orgasm & I'm not sure
these fake eyelashes from Duane Reade
are cruelty-free to the man who desires me but
I depend on an air of violence
to cherish more, calm down. Still
please don't nailgun me
again in my sleep tonight.
Interred in the dripping woods of
the blue elves of the 80's
metabolizing their rejection
openly & then in teams, yay!
I want to be in a boi gang
in the worst way. I'd like to be
"carried" in a fetish film. You
think you could love me? You
love me in your dreams you better
wake up & apologize.

BRAT

I am all about heavenly cavorting
here on silly earth.
& I misbehave around death
& I tug on trouble's braids.
but tonight I am going to pretend
I know the people who love me.

TASHI DELEK.

for Darragh, I miss you.

The gentle blanching of somebody charging
expired, sans Visa & sans culottes -
as if the Incredible Hulk burst
dizzily through a wallpaper of watercolors
to be as accepted & integrated as a newbie
at a 12-step meeting on fire for his Higher Power,
i.e., a sorority rush of brushfires in a field of bluets.
Later, chords for a key you can't even scream in
& worse, the crabbed script of a kindred composer
for notes you just can't reach standing gingerly
on your own crumbling sandbar. But like lasagna
made from moist puppychow at a 3/4 house,
"We take what's given with gratitude."
"In times of crisis, we must all decide
again & again whom we love" & I choose you & You & YOU.
You slept with my husband — I choose you.
You raped me in the shallow waters — I choose you.
You wrecked my skater bangs with wig shampoo — I choose you.
You pressured my morphine heart sans hospice — I choose you
too. Even in death, I choose you & in times
of crisis, I choose you again & again because
we outlaws take care of our own.

TEENS OF DARING, CUT THE TUNGSTEN LIGHTS.

after the "Billy the Kid" documentary

Anything I swear to you is an alibi
for something true. I speak in Heart,
fooling nobody. You better use your Nikes
as I know the stealthy back way to your pain
since I am a future angel or whatever.
I guess this is the way that everything
evil happens, like tonight. This girl
knew a boi who "threw down" for Robert
Kennedy weeping on a white stair
in the Year of Our Lord 1968. Crazy, sorry,
crazy, sorry, crazy, sorry. Everything
I drunkenly text is true, all 56 crayons:
"Pimples are sexy & funerals are neat."
"I'll go put these in some rubbing alcohol."
"It's beautiful that you are tight."
I suppose you black out after you take in
a fairly small amount of love & my inhaler
just up & died. Isn't it enough that there
is blood on the floor & that I am on my way,
barking, "Nothing, the world, nobody can be trusted?"
Please cast shadows with your eyelashes tomorrow
so it'll be better, since, let's face it,
everybody leaves.

THE PILL BOOK

DEPAKOTE

I felt most at home on this pill in a bucolic shire
of the Hamptons amid the piss-colored braids
of wheat on a Metamucil can, milkweed & sneeze drops,
a track The Loneliness of a Middle Distance Runner
never checked out in the Orangeade foam of dawn.
Glistening like a brow in an aspirin ad on the telly,
I've got a brain like soaked coral.
I've got a tongue like a baby's penis.
I'm Bruce Willis in The Sixth Sense –
I'm dead but I don't know it.
My pen, my Eskimo blood spilled cheekily
over good & dear people. I managed to write this
by myself With a Little Help from My Friends.
When I said, "Oh get me away I'm dying,"
I meant I wanted a cigarette & a problem child
on a peony-filled evening. In the dry heat
of photocopy fans, making Easter cards with the, uh,
terminally ill, you hold the retinal scanner to my heart.
"Now I know how Joan of Arc felt
as flames rose to her Roman nose &
her hearing aid began to melt..."
And in the darkened underpass I gave
blood & now my French is shaky.

KLONOPIN

A jillion dirty Larrys rise from the dead,
unheeding, & grope with bandaged fingers
toward the brass section of The Climax Band.
Why was his melancholy oyster heart still
running? Crack open this ribcage for your
stale dessert. But darkness ain't sweet
& Love Goes On Anyway. Heart Failed
in the Back of a Taxi! My Nescafe is burning
down my throat & through my breasts. I imagine
the voluptuousness of death & its filthy
alma mater. But humidity makes Baby Jesus cry.
Snow cuts my wrists & Montauk no longer exists —
just mosquitoes electrified, slurping
your anemic blood black as creosote.
The unbelievable noon will move you,
undo you, like a frozen blue fetus
in the open palm of the sun.

XANAX

Ave Maria, walk in beauty & bring me
a Samuel Adams beer. I said, "Ya Hey,
walk in beauty!" But isn't there always
a "beige hallway" type person achingly alive
or lionized by janitors, with a band
of descending seraphim hurling bolts,
soft & fierce like an arrow from the arsenal
of Cupid? Act now & receive these lovely
Ginzu knives. See, I don't know what's worse:
my karma or my credit. Throw me a bone
& I'll demand a skeleton. Guess I'll just sleep
my way to the middle, wear my coronary
on my sleeve, sushi-pink & thundering away
like the uptown 6. Rats. Fortunately I don't
have on my Rag & Bone jeans. Now why should I
suddenly plop down & color manga?
Troublingly gorgeous as a child swollen
with rain, sitting shiva over our love
which translates: I live in damnation,
you: next to it.

PAXIL

If I had a million dollars, I mean
if it weren't all tied up in securities,
I'd give all the poets 2 weeks in Pacific
Daylight Time. For serious. Sometimes

I romanticize the proletariat. Other quarters,
I join trophy wives poolside: human tempura
banging White Russians back to back & in the moonlight,
the oleanders look like bosoms heaving

drowsily over the inexperienced lake. Wait,
I swear I am coming they keep whispering…
Your come: teeth-whitening serum or a snail's trail
across a sack of ice under Goan strobe lights,

as sticky & heavy as Asian rice & about as candid
as a Masonic lodge. Or as personal as a Nerve ad:
"Zero abortions, zero dependents, & financially secure
in a quasi-geisha way." Corks bob in our wine

like the pageboys on the women on Park
as an Amstel sun burns over a flock of
buildings. Your eyes are the green pools
of drowned toddlers, your kneecaps -

the skulls of inbred dogs, your penis
which resembles a sunburned baby's arm
& smells of chlorine brings me to —
tears? No, thank you awfully much,

it's positively rain. Me, I'm strong,
can do the Hercules One Arm Bed-to-Bed Transfer
but can't lift too much anymore without feeling
dirty. Please take out the garbage of this poem &

if you've ever read a poem this bad,
then welcome back.

LAMICTAL

I felt my body take a leaf of absence—
the real "me" having absconded into a Swiss
waterfall, as glossy as the family silver or
a glimpse of Ibiza on which I sailed along
in a dream. I tell everyone I drowned
in the tuna redness of the morning,
in the cornflake slush of leaves. My mood
ring blacked out. Would you like a Sanka?
Pee on my lap & whisper brand-name bicycles
in my ear. In a fog stubbled with buildings
& what have you, veins in the trees tense
like Baryshnikov's arms & then the menthol
climax of a hot pill thrust down the throat
of an ice sculpture. As Tuesday's rain is falling
on the clientele, heavy as a lead dental cape
on my chest, I am a packet of powdered sea monkeys
& you act like water. But my aquarium broke
& these days are just like melted Toblerone.

LITHIUM

after David Shapiro

Sweetie said, "I want you very much."
Do you believe in this fabulous affair?
White mustard, the orgasm came rushing out
of nowhere, like sudden, drunk party guests.
Where is my French bottled water?
And then balloons, helium-filled strays
traipsing around the ski clinic. Rescue me
from this Procrustean bed. I have no godfather -
only the occasional vitamin-stuffed hustler
& heaven, full of the terminally ill. But chiefly
I refer to variations in brilliance. What have you
got roughly in your breast? A condominium
of tony desire & your bright red tears,
Chekhovian, yes? I press toward your dirt siesta,
sobbing amid fireflies, impossible to enter
like hailing a taxi on an ice floe in the Arctic
wearing white. Could the author of Jim Dine
please stand up? There is correction fluid,
an ambulance waiting in the arboretum.

ABILIFY

It's a Christ-awful small affair
for the boi with the mousy hair.
Having stiffed the waitress at Truck's Famous,
I am no longer a living poet (consumption)
just the plaything of collection agencies
& subpoena artists. Right. So the last brothers
of bangers & mash, the American South,
sucking the sherbets from my blah idea of romance.
The campus dryheads — they left me for dead.
Some motion in ganglands stabbed me down.
But there's this hottish way of looking
where you just marvel, confess: Yeah, I smoke a lot,
felt real bad about The Tar Baby as a child.

MERIDIA

Real men dangle their modifiers
on a perp walk, but sexuality is fluid.
Soda runs like the River Jordan
at Popeye's Chicken & manna is as good
for the munchies as scalding hors d'oeuvres
at funeral wake. The sweaty slaying
of dragons & nicotine epiphanies
& so forth since I switched from Diet
to Coke Zero. Eking out lyfe with panic
pills & Swiss bank accounts, I took your soul
out waltzing into the night. Your quiet
passing caught the light. I believe
Dorian Gray had a purple heart.
We're all the same height lying down.

LIKE A LAKE TOUCHING 4 STATES BUT
NOT GETTING ANY OF THEM WET

A TINY FAN OF SAILOR UNIFORMS

For a good time, I misunderstood The Promise so
please feel free to snort my ashes. I decidedly
hope many of you are twittering tonight about
your experience with my human coke, this powdered
imp in a splash zone. Scratch that, Splendor
in the Grass, how can I slip inside your cramped
arabesque when I flunked both geometry & joinery
on scholarship? Each night a rich dust settles.
Carnal nosebleeds & the Vermeers are way intense.

ANY NUMBER CAN DIE!

"Dude, we have kidnapped your acedia.
Further details later." OMG! So funny.
I did it with fab shades on & diamonds.
Always shocked, I'd rather not play. It's
been a long time since I've gamely run
through dark lawns uninvited. I'd rather
turn gold sleeping in the sun. Stay gold.
Don't Let the Sun Go Down on Your
Grievances. We are not profane, we have
been profaned. Bambini, out here, on my own
I subscribed to Several-Variable Calculus.
But wait! What are you doing with such
a long rope? I am studying for the bar.
Yes, I am taking the bar very seriously
but now I just want to look at pretty things
& watch the Skylab Liftoff. I know Freud,
I know he is Viennese & very important. I
constantly police my feelings: Don't canonize.
Don't be idiotically self-destructive. We are
not profane. I am saving myself for my Father.
Truck, that's sick. I meant God. No, no please,
go ahead. It's an original sin, but please
feel free to touch it. My discomfort is radical
& I am counting on Europe to fix that, so help me
God, weather the first, worst wave of shame.
Arterials in the baking Acropolis heat,
breathing your vernal hair, the loosenings
of "why," the fragrances of bleeding,
the bloodletting softly, the antifreeze
of summer, the smell of warm toast & I am
counting on Europe to fix me. After I have
wrested your spirit from Richard Hell &
installed you at the Plaza, "real lyfe,"
as I understand it, is not about breeding
& believing in rigidity, but the blue flower,
"le bleu fleur?" At the end of this summer,
after you leave, I will not be able
to speak a word of French.

BAISERS

for A.S.

July, the cot of a child carried off
by an epidemic, I met you starving
in a place of Biblical crimes, buzzing
heat flies. Sitting in a dark thatch
suite with a flute of champagne, my hand
trembles, distracted by gunfire sometimes.
Quarantined & suffering solo, your dark
animal radiance burns like a soft brain
napping in tough bone. Summer feels like
an overwarm sickroom with pinky swears
forever & a phone number to call if
the pony runs dry. I think your face
is a minority in my heart & God will
help me resist your pageant body.
The riot of fauna, you have to ride
something. I have christened my orbiter
& landing vehicle Rocketgrrl & Spider.
I am afraid of leaving the States & yet
I forgive myself enough to leave again.
My instinct is broken, please sign my cast.
On my night table: The Peanuts Treasury &
The Book of Nods. If you cut a tragic figure,
I'll salt you with lime. I declare myself
a nation of zero under a Yuletide mantle
of kisses. I am a tiny & fundamentally
ridiculous person. And I drive a stick.

BLACK BALLOON

Isn't it crazy that Last Night a DJ Saved My Lyfe,
that Sakharov created the bomb & that we chew on
each other's genitals? A minor friar of chastity
& obedience, my faith is full frontal with stunt
men on fire, the works. You've dented my lunatic
belief in the future. Frazzled, male children pat
the earth, of course they do. I record rituals
to give grief form, of course I do. My loins act
like a Chia Pet when you neglect them. A hybrid of
gauze & puffy toothpaste, these are kawaii clouds
in dark days of floating teddy boys, miscreants
in tow. I smoke, I tan, I drink, I puncture
the time warp continuum with shivs, Chex Mix
for guests under the influence. Thank you so awfully
much for your time & consideration, but before I
let you go today, I'd like to schedule a celluloid
screening of how the atoms misbehave inside when
you speak that way to me. I can't get through
to you, this alone. But I can get through, alone.

BLOODSHOT'S BIG DAY OFF.

With only 2 status refreshes about the victims
of the Molasses Disaster, I'm so "hardcore" I
ejaculate blood in the slums of Midtown Manhattan,
then sleaze by the Strawberry prom-dress giveaway.
Every welded gold crown has an impoverished owner
with teeth, a coronet of seed pearls. If bipolar
spending doesn't get you, violence will. Does Mister
President care about our starlets getting eaten
alive? I wish to be eaten alive & often, cool.
I wish to be a member of an extinct, hobbit-like
species of miniature humanoids attending the Astor
fortune trial with the big guns. Ukrainian Roulette.
Bang. Damn, a blank. Like a lake touching 4 states
but not getting any of them wet. Let's be clear:
I.Would.Like.An.Auditory.Appendage.Of.Corn.
Please.Don't.Give.Up.And.Find.Peace.

BOHEMIAN HEIGHTS

Screamingly carnal, my Bird of Paradise, I
would place you on a first-class Audubon
Society postage stamp & mail you home. But
then, because so much formal perfection can
be chilling, the man who mistook his wife for
Greenland's melting ice cap springs forward,
falls back, no further past viral pandemics
& dirty bombshells. Fetchingly disheveled birds
need help to become comfortably modern American
flyers like Howard Hughes, but at least he had
planes to get out. This is my bird problem, brown
bellied & driven out of the park by Christo's wife.
The labial petals you bruise underfoot are beaded
with dew to avoid wasting even a nanosecond of
birdable daylight. It's something to be anxious
about, if you want to be anxious about something.
Writing checks to the Children's Welfare League,
the Sierra Club, your delta heart in winter is too
beautiful to stay embarrassed inside for long. I
scribble toxic jeremiads about alpine bohemia while
the windows are darkening but it's a point of pride
with me never to write secondary literature when resting
my pulse rate below 30 these dark days without you.

BRONZE MEDALS

I want a boyfriend so when he's wicked old
I can watch the late sun glow salmon-bright
through the cartilage of his ginormous hairy ears
while we sneeze together on a plank bench
amid flowering dogwood. But I would settle
for a string of meaningless affairs, graciously
resigned like mezzanine disappointment
when you'd badly hoped for closeness.

CLOSER

Hiccup & the yogurt infant skull
enters this world already knowing
how to blind gerbils with refrigerator
light & we keep on like that, touching
each other professionally until it hurts
just right. Keep losing control of your
functions & I will, yeah, notice but
ditch you for the cute mourner with
the red howl up front. The crust of stars
burning naively - our soufflé of nights
to believe in. Lushed out in the hush
of Meyer lemon groves, I hang on your
voice, still, like a noose, anchored
by stale weight. With the stink of
expiration heavier than horseshoe crab
shells in a damp sauna, I am missing you
but not to excess, close to nothing at all.

RIVER OF TIME

What's with the midnight shades?
Casper, I got photosensitivity.
Secondary, my peepers are too dark.
Tertiary, I'm destroyed by Lady Di
murals, nibbled by rain, fake love
with its patina of compassion.
Quadrary, I'm branching out blindly,
with the hesitancy of a bonsai tree.
My mother bore a knife, a gay blade
with no spring-release. There is nowhere
safe to live when you are dangerous.
So many right turns at 3 in the morning,
I am just some water ride at Epcot
that is educational but not much fun
& doesn't make anyone wet. Let's
call a moratorium on casual loving.
Cloaked in a white lab coat in Community
Outreach, my lust? It's like half-retarded.
"How about the other half?"

GREY ATOMS

A custodian of a dirty & dwindling angst, I won
my Oscar at a young age for my dramatic
re-enactment of the brutal comic implication
of being, a still that flatlined us all. Now I
retreat to my trailer to memorize lines
for execution. Let me hold my breath inside
you when they make me walk the narrow line.
At which point, you become all sweetness & light.
I wish to be arrested in a Windsor Light Condensed.
But instead, armed only with a gold Sharpie, I
hover above the function row, bleeding through
like watercolors in the rain, consoling my friend:
Aw, babe, no, that's not a pimple, that's a gunshot wound.

I AM THE CHEESE, DUH.

I am the cheese, the sandwich
in your backpack for over a year
now. We had a future together

& now we don't because you let
my heat & age get to you. In heat,
I see you are a tiny fan of function.

I personally am a fan of form & ruin.
Drawing connections at the same time
decrying them. I have a wailing wall

that drunk teens arouse with dry
cleaning. Like a Greek pledge
with pepper spray & the safety

off, I am miserable & moronic
in my protective training bra.
Beneath your coronic gaze my tiny

chest hurts. I see Waldo all sketched
out in your left pupil. So what's
my prize? Because I'm here for

a prize, y'know? I'm no kid.
I'm just some science project
but chances are I'm gonna want

a glass of milk. I will probably
ask for 2%, a straw. Plaster me
together in a fury of nutrition

before we strike out. Are you
sure you are okay Living Only
For the City? I commend you

on catering to my confusion.
Still, it's nice to know the sex
of the children before you escort

them to the lavatory. Somebody
maybe should have told Henry
Darger that. Just saying.

IN THE WILD WHITE CONDO,

a little rusty sleigh bell is our stimulus
package. Scotland's sheep shrink while my
pensmenship improves, grows insane, foaming
up through pores that let the chill inside. If
you don't shiver always, even in July, then
I can't call you my own cherished black growth.
I led my innocent groom down the wrong track:
water lilies, deathhhhhhh, a shawl of teardrops
for the hot children shot through with only skim.
Even damply outlined in the Caucasian Chalk
Circle, throbs more of a pulse than we have now,
tagged as a seemingly single thing like a nun
we pass on the street & stare at but don't feel.
We hunt for a good shepherd's pie, grabbing a slice
on Avenue of the Americas, I told you: I am, I said,
begging you, I said, it's hot—I feel some pain.

KINK, EVIL, RELIGION, LOVE.

Everyone has their heart blown in high school
by The Stranger. My obsession floating politely
in the background, I would like to occupy France.
Your iambic feet stink of defeat, so hot my French

accent sinks in the mid-Atlantic. I qualify for
lunch assistance & am at risk. But I met a nurse
I could die for. It's negritude, it's heroin,
an acquired taste like vampirism. Every time

his pretty fangs pop out, pretty young thang,
steam pours from my laptop. Press the reward
valve for pleasure pellets, little skate rat.
Scratch & sniff the elusive base-level reality

of a superstar. "Truck, my wife must see something
special in you," says a man of God over dessert.
How did you know my Christian name? My lung
collapses spiritually in Montmartre. Stinging

& bold, I try yoga to break out of panic.
My exposé tape partially ruined by sirens,
I am held hostage in the unclothed corner
of your tiredness, when really I just wanted

to use your wading pool. A Dirt Devil for my
spiritual vacuum, you act shocked but not
floored by the giant crater in the bedroom.
I tolerate your fear of chemistry sets just so

you'll let me climb your treehouse. Elephant
Man's bones, hyperbaric chambers, Evian on tap.
Outlaw loner but he could dance. Somewhere far
south of zero, I adore you, while the shut-in inside

the hurt locker, the Beretta Boi, puts the moves
on hunters with guns. Latisse, please remember
the safe word is "Latisse." Hershey ink for your eye
fringe & destruction from Heaven above, smudged

at dusk & smarting. Twee kids, the Tang of today, shiver
beneath your fluttery, fevered touch. Children of the Corn
die by Korn in the cul-de-sac of Pizza Hut, an abstract
plume of fallout boys feathering toward Gay Paree.

LES FEUILLES MORTES

for Iggy Pop

The possibility of an island
looms stately over a sea of sludge
where Bic lighters aloft are stunt
doubles for meteorites smelling
faithfully of Old Gold & Aqua Net.
Do we embrace the 38 Special?
Tongue-tied, broken, & demonic,
strings are the ultimate crutch,
but I gently draw the line at horns.
Please manipulate my morning words
with compassion, compression & reverb
to lend me character.

LIGHT MERIT

Attempting to shock pastels brighter
with the heart paddles, yelling "Clear,"
some gang of ghosts has me in a deadlock.
Shades of summer camp & a bored counselor
neglecting the tutored stars of track & field.
Where have all the bright ones gone? Fading fast,
the constantly new darks. Even this is lifted,
a sketch of an overweight trunk in the afternoon
of today. Like birthday sex, we strain wildly
to choose the brand of our gross ruin. Hotels
hugged with brittle ivy, snow. You will marry
this town & I will grow old in the breweries,
in the hills flecked with piss. Hoping the express
ramp but sensing broken stares. Please, dammit,
back gently out of the hosiery, snag nothing
flying past you, the adult legs en route to work.
I've been moved, or moved us, or I have simply
moved away without notice.

MANSIONS IN RUIN

Recluses should have 2 feet
sawed off the bottom
of the apartment door. Meth
doesn't upset parents the way
spinsterdom does. Like mansions
in ruin, I am drowsy
but welcoming impact. You know
I can still rally back,
maybe. I'm not concerned
for not knowing the intent
of my crowd. I'll grow back,
thicker, denser, more deeply
than cheap electrolysis. Hissing
pipes in the boiler room
is just my anatomy saying, "Hi!"
to you. I don't love you but I
need you physically to see me
through. My dreads dangle
like garlands from my brain.
For a boi in heat, I can't
even get hard anymore. Spike
my Shirley Temple with teardrops
that taste like rat poison,
that shock me to a tabernacle.
Give me something I can hate.
Give me something I can feel.

MORE OR LESS FORSWORN.

I prefer mint juleps in the Oval Office over stale
fiefdoms. The fuzz shuttered the Marquee, hazel
cartoon tears welling up in Harlem, Castro, Mission,

Emerald City. Yes, I've used a bong & precious gems,
a primer for ladyboys to resist breastfeeding while
drunk. Dark horse, stick out your chest to be fair.

I need to mandate paid maternity leave of you. Cabbage
roses & John Kale are thriving in my floral bed where
my soul is composted with a loamy mix of crank &

St.-Tropez browns. Insulated by grownup leftover mom
jeans, you make my irrigation system fail visible.
I am wearing the bloody patchwork pelts of many poems

I had to kill to not catch pneumonia standing next to
you, though even torpedo attacks on the Ottoman Empire
couldn't keep me away. Still in my brain I swear we

were having Queen Blizzards that year on the bleachers.
I throw down for members of The Weather Underground.
"I'm a perfect little snowflake!" (You aren't.) And

now the biggest pyrotechnic display in the South
is just Pop Rocks in my mouth. I am a friend of Iran
but sniff the Lebanese Blonde in a Ziploc bag, pucker

up. No wet paste of pet waste please. I need a child
translator, sharkfood money to know the limit of my X
as he approaches infinity, an aeration drill to poke

holes in the pile of shit I'm in to see out. As gentle
as carrot rape when you've forsworn Big Macs at dusk,
I tap a small prince with deadstock enamel crowns to

touch up my celebrity with the Rackets Bureau. Virgin
fiber bursting nu-metal eardrums, I fancy making noise
today. So many people in the neighborhood.

PLASMA'S JUST WEAK SAUCE ANYWAY

Post-prandial, you must color the film
of the ibises alone in the green room
tonight. I-I'm going out like a light,
lightly but, little Niagara of affliction,
what reason have you to throw down so early,
not enough proper nouns for blood anymore?
Sweet & nestled tight in a kelp curl like
incubated chew in the bulbous cheeks of
Dizzy, I believe in sanctuary for those
washed up. I believe that in the rectory
of Neptune, children stay free. I see
into fields of thyme when I switch tracks
hunting for something less swollen & Zion
switches amusement parks on me, feigning
tube rides on one of the most crowded
breaks in the world like the crude blue pasta
of a preemie's intestines shrilly offered
as a tiny new human salad with a birthday.
The shadows of my locs lengthen in late sun
faster than the lines of widows in safety vests
queued around the corner for Lethe. You're
a full moon, stay up, clutch the brownies
to your ruby-teated chest & stink proudly.

PLEASE ENJOY YOUR STAY

To whoever's been fuming in the lavatory,
this message is for you. If you continue
to fume, you will, believe me, find out
who you are, & when you do, we will tuck
you softly in. The down comforter of art,
your crash pad, will receive you in free,
good shape. We, the executors of your comfort,
will mist your temples with kisses & mint
moist wipes, calm you down with comics,
Rimbaud, & Xanax while you fume in Babylon
until the next tuck-in at dusk. Thanks
for adjusting your tears to an objective
aperture. Grace & peace to you on earth
which is where we convulse, freezing
but privileged to be among the sensate,
welcome without single supplement fees.

PROMHEART

I feel the tension of piano wire tonight
like an air palace preserved in lungs
of industrial-grade chicken-barbed glass.

Steal tapas from a baby king, end up
in an underground supermax, uptown
dowagers crying their blue ovaries off,

hearts as true as a cornfield but as flammable.
Powdered geishas calm me down while I rest
on withered laurels in my head. I hate

Friday nights, too many shadow players
from back in the shame days to see what
Goethe was hiding, the thunder underneath,

knowing it, feeling it, a sawed-off fishpriest
cocked at this lush lyfe, anxiety worming
its way to the curb before my foot gets there.

The midnight skeleton staff outnumbers those
starving in the condensation on freezer doors.
Eyes sauced but acrylic-bright like 2 cherries

floating on a kid's pancake, lacquered down
with emotional violence, I know my .22s.
The soft pop screaming at me as if volume

increased comprehension for a deaf man
moving a credenza at Rose of Sharon on Essex
and I need a paraffin test. The caper on cruise

control in The Air-Conditioned Nightmare penned
by Henry Miller. See these left wing galleys,
what you're looking at right now doesn't even exist.

In pristine wrappers & inscribed, "Honor Among Thieves,"
in gladiator school, I am smarting about curfew,
those hairy fists. Quality of Life shows up

about as timely as a past-life regression
therapist. Outline molded in frost on the glass
doors, I see the Torah page you're standing on.

The bloodred crescents throbbing from behind,
lighting us up from here to the river Styx.
Leaving a kitchen wall with jaundiced twin stars

of David, shafts of dustmoon coursing through
the clefts: Its nowness, its right here and nowness.
In the lee of that wall. I'm my own kid.

TRUE PATRON OF THE ARTS

As I work on my needlepoint, certified near
colorless, somewhere a sailor made of young
spinach fights to the death just for the wine
list. I bet the D.A. could drink a case like
him at a slumber party raffle for the homeless
with Booze, Ammo, Muesli & the runner up wins
a seminal shift to wear on holiday in Andalucia.
Thank Almighty God for British Imperialism
so that wherever we go, we are sort of almost
home. We have fled by now 1,000 plus years
through the desert, a lot of it very recently.
I insist now we are going to shower in kisses
& dry vermouth from the mouth of one of the most
violently anemic shut-ins in the territory. But
I believe you could love her. I believe you could
finish her off with your warm, tan farm hands.

WHILE I WAS IN THE DOGHOUSE,

the Red Baron sang madrigals during thermals
tearing off the roof, hit these glorious 9
high C's pouring down on me, so when I think
of Purple Rain, Prince, I think of lace & air
guitar riffs, how my lucky Challenger aircraft
coin holds the same wack valence as bloodshot
Gatsby paddling a dinghy against the current
in a sea colony where the office gestalt thrives
hawkish & pullulating with Bluetooth & kennel
cough. By the way, I speak the Queen's English
& can get you home safely too, any port in a storm.

WHY OCEANOGRAPHY, MISS DIDION?

Tidal heritage, sweetheart.
I am ceaselessly involved.
People are always introducing me
to their glaring pet peeves.
The Sun's Big Day Off is just
a solar eclipse sometimes.
Can two people eclipse each
other without blocking the light?
Hence, I think my doorman makes me
cry on acid. You find nothing but
unnamed doors opening then being
slammed shut, i.e. Lactic Acid
Build Up, the way you "build"
a drink of Absinthe, a little
bit green, a bit absently. I die
laughing. I do.

SIGIL

Middle finger to the clusters of haters!
Terror skies deftly enough through the course
of our blood in a vacuum without their help.
For a boi without both oars in the water &
eagerly darting into violent vistas, of my always
pulsing onward: the starry water propels me.
The fudge blackness dotted with nautical pulp
is my dazzling summer Mustang. The key to keeping on
is usually the ignition key. Like hairspray
on a fart, draughts of myrrh enflame us
in our Catholic need. Lilac shafts bathe us
in the recognition of home, of the slackening
of the umbilical cord like a belt coming casually
off when microbes of lust gather on a sigil
before removing the assonance of the anthem:
All together! Ice cream, you scream, we all scream:
I am together, so together, perfectly postured,
upright but not uptight. Under cloudbursts
of crisis & on my back staring up at the roof
of the church, this boi, stalwart, flying
with conviction, the way Jet Blue loves
its Mormons, spirits them home. No man,
an island. Each girl, a planet.